ideals® CHRISTMAS

Glad Christmas comes, and every hearth
Makes room to give him welcome now. . . .
Neighbors resume their annual cheer,
Wishing, with smiles and spirits high,
Glad Christmas and a happy year
To every morning passerby.
—JOHN CLARE

IDEALS PUBLICATIONS

NASHVILLE, TENNESSEE

Signs of Christmas
Lucille King

Carols singing, church bells ringing,
It's Christmastime again.
Wind a-blowing, hearth fires glowing,
Candles shine in windowpanes.

Pine and holly, fir and hemlock,
A bunch of mistletoe or more;
Skaters skating, children laughing,
A jolly snowman by the door.

White-capped roofs and horses' hooves
Clattering o'er a crusted snow;
Sleigh bells jingling, store bells tinkling
As the shoppers come and go.

Candy canes and crowded lanes,
Goodwill and peace to men;
All around, this spirit abounds—
It's Christmastime again.

Stocking Stuffer
Elizabeth Collier

Christmas fills the senses
In a most delicious way.
The sight and sound and taste of it
For one full month hold sway.
Crisp and brittle holly wreaths,
Candles' velvet glow,
The smell of cookies baking,
The crunch of sparkling snow,
The eyes of little children
A-shine with hope and joy,
The shimmer of the Christmas tree,
Its base all banked with toys.
Christmas fills the senses, true,
But this is just a part;
For even more than all the rest,
Christmas fills the heart.

Song for Christmas
Sudie Stuart Hager

I love the Yuletide's radiant things—
The treetop angel's spun-glass wings,
Each scarlet ball and tinseled limb,
The tapers sputtering, soft and dim,
The light in happy children's eyes,
A bright-faced doll that talks and cries,
The log that sparkles on the grate,
The glow that follows through the gate,
A neighboring window's candle-wreath,
The snow, like burnished gold, beneath,
And the sky, bright-jeweled o'erhead,
As on that night above His bed.

Photograph by Dianne Dietrich Leis/Dietrich Photography

Christmas Is the Best Day of Winter

Rosalyn Hart Finch

Winter came boldly to town again this year, frosting the clammy streets and sifting bleary halos around the pole lights. Wrapped in cold, nose-stinging air, winter brushed its frosty hands all over the trees, favoring none more than others. Nude branches, as well as the plushy, needle-covered fir limbs, are exquisite in their ice-lustered spangles.

Here and there happy souls take secret little slides, adults choosing out-of-the-way spots, youngsters daring on the very face of the town itself. The crisp air enters the bloodstream as instant, invigorating current, urging one to walk out among the newly revealed secrets kept hidden all summer long—shaggy, high-rise bird apartments nested overhead; shiny red berries decorating withered brown forest limbs; the winding, seeking, formerly green-shrouded courses of creek and river now swelling ice-clad shoulders to their banks.

We are all charged with expectations, for we know that winter's specialty, heavy snowfall, is not far away. Does the snow fail to stir any of our imaginations? Or will we merely gaze in awe at its dazzling descent, remembering similar times of wonder? Won't that nameless feeling of pleasure we all experience at suddenly awakening to a fresh, soft, white world brighten some of the humdrum hours of living and put a new face on dispositions?

Certainly, during the holiday season, winter interweaves a jovial spirit into everything. It puts

A snow-covered barn in Hebron, New Hampshire. Photograph by William H. Johnson

a bloom on the cheeks of small fry and oldsters alike. Folks look healthier with their ruddy complexions. Cheerful tones and happy words crowd the air, bidding to outdo one another.

Even indoors, winter exerts its delicious side effects. Domesticity takes on fresh charm with burning logs snapping in the fireplace, their glow reflected in the faces of our loved ones. Slippered feet prop contentedly on couches and footstools. Small sips of steaming hot cocoa or coffee seem to contain soothing spirits of tranquilizing secrets.

Yes, winter is here. Thank God for winter. Without her we might never have been introduced to the thoroughly delightful meaning of coziness.

Now in winter's clutches we are not struggling, for we look to her highest pinnacle, Christmas. Christmas is the best day of winter and of the whole year for most of us. On this day we will call to our minds and hearts the very tenderest of thoughts about friends far and near. On this day we will feel able to consider forgiveness for all our past hurts, big and little. We will ferret out large supplies of generosity that have lain dormant throughout the rest of the year and spread them graciously around town.

Christmas will be followed with a forward-looking attitude for the coming new year. Resolutions will be made in winter's presence to do better deeds with less faltering during the years ahead, to move, each in his own way, toward peace for all the world over.

Aren't we glad that winter came again to town this year? This wonderful, unchanging order in our changing, disordered world must indeed be a comforting balm to us all. Merry Christmas!

Sometime During Christmas

Ree Reaney

Sometime during Christmas
As the days go rushing by,
Take time to see the Christmas lights
Mist-haloed 'gainst the sky.

Sometime during Christmas
Breathe deep the Christmas smell;
The bayberry and the piney scents;
What welcome they foretell!

Sometime during Christmas
When carolers are singing,
Retell the age-old story
For which the bells are ringing.

Sometime during Christmas
Midst the gaiety and noise,
Take time to hear the quietness
Of simple Christmas joys.

Sometime during Christmas
Remember friends are near,
And feel the warmth of knowing
That your friendship's very dear!

The First Snow

Eileen Spinelli

The first snow
falls
softly.
Suddenly
moonlit children
spill across
the sidewalks
laughing.
Give me
your red-mittened hand.
We will join them.
The moon
will light
our faces too.
It is time that
we learn again
the play
and the magic
of peace
in that first snow
that falls.

Family ·Recipes

Snowy Day Chocolate Cookie Cheesecake

2	cups chocolate sandwich cookie crumbs	2	tablespoons all-purpose flour
2	tablespoons butter, melted	2¾	teaspoons vanilla extract, divided
¼	cup packed brown sugar	4	eggs
½	teaspoon ground cinnamon	1½	cups chocolate sandwich cookie pieces
2	pounds cream cheese, softened	16	ounces sour cream
1½	cups granulated sugar, divided	1	cup semisweet chocolate chips
1	cup heavy whipping cream, divided		

Preheat oven to 350°F. In a medium bowl, combine 2 cups cookie crumbs, melted butter, brown sugar, and cinnamon. Firmly press mixture evenly onto bottom and 1 inch up sides of a 9-inch springform pan. Bake 5 minutes; remove from oven and set aside.

In a large bowl, beat cream cheese until smooth. Gradually mix in 1¼ cups sugar, ⅓ cup whipping cream, flour, and 1 teaspoon vanilla. Add eggs, one at a time, beating after each addition. Pour ⅓ of batter into prepared pan. Top with cookie pieces; pour in remaining batter. Bake 45 minutes. Remove from oven and set aside.

In a medium bowl, combine sour cream, ¼ cup sugar, and 1 teaspoon vanilla; spread evenly on cheesecake. Bake 7 minutes; turn oven off and leave cheesecake in oven 30 minutes. Remove from oven and cool completely in pan on a wire rack.

In a small saucepan over low heat, combine ⅔ cup whipping cream and chocolate chips; stir until chocolate melts. Stir in ¾ teaspoon vanilla; mix well. Drizzle warm mixture over cheesecake and refrigerate at least 8 hours. About ½ to 1 hour before serving, remove cheesecake from refrigerator and remove ring from springform pan. Garnish as desired and serve. Makes 10 to 12 servings.

White Christmas Hot Cocoa

2 cups whipping cream
6 cups milk
1 teaspoon vanilla extract
1 teaspoon peppermint extract, optional

1 (12-ounce) package white or milk
   chocolate chips
   Whipped topping or marshmallows
10 candy canes or peppermint sticks

In a slow cooker, stir together the whipping cream, milk, vanilla, peppermint extract (if desired), and white or milk chocolate chips. Cover and cook on low for 2 to 2½ hours, stirring occasionally, until mixture is hot and chocolate chips are melted. Stir and ladle into mugs; top with whipped topping or marshmallows and garnish with candy canes or peppermint sticks. Makes 10 servings.

Molasses Sugar Cookies

4 cups all-purpose flour
4 teaspoons baking soda
2 teaspoons ground cinnamon
1 teaspoon ground cloves
1 teaspoon ground ginger
1 teaspoon salt

1½ cups shortening
1 cup light brown sugar
1 cup granulated sugar
2 eggs
½ cup molasses
   Red and green colored sugars

In a large bowl, sift together flour, baking soda, cinnamon, cloves, ginger, and salt. Set aside. In a medium saucepan, melt shortening; allow to cool. Add granulated and brown sugars, eggs, and molasses; beat well. Add to dry ingredients. Mix well and chill, covered, at least 3 hours.

Preheat oven to 375°F. Form dough into walnut-size balls. Roll in colored sugars. Place about 2 inches apart on an ungreased cookie sheet and bake 8 to 10 minutes. Remove from pan and cool on wire racks; store in an airtight container. Makes 6 dozen cookies.

A Dear Little Schemer

Mary Mapes Dodge

There was a little daughter once whose feet were oh-so-small
That when the Christmas Eve came round, they wouldn't do at all.
At least she said they wouldn't do, and so she tried another's,
And folding her wee stocking up, she slyly took her mother's.

"I'll pin this big one here," she said, then sat before the fire,
Watching the supple, dancing flames and shadows darting by her;
Till silently she drifted off to that queer land, you know,
Of "Nowhere in Particular" where sleepy children go.

She never knew the tumult rare that came upon the roof!
She never heard the patter of a single reindeer hoof;
She never knew how Some One came and looked his shrewd surprise
At the wee foot and the stocking—so different in size!

She only knew, when morning dawned, that she was safe in bed.
"It's Christmas! Ho!" and merrily she raised her pretty head;
Then, wild with glee, she saw what "dear Old Santa Claus" had done
And ran to tell the joyful news to each and every one!

"Mama! Papa! Please come and look! A lovely doll, and all!"
And "See how full the stocking is! Mine *would* have been too small.
I borrowed this for Santa Claus. It isn't fair, you know,
To make him wait forever for a little girl to grow."

Day Before Christmas
Marchette Chute

We have been helping with the cake
And licking out the pan
And wrapping up our packages
As neatly as we can.
And we have hung our stockings up
Beside the open grate,
And now there's nothing more to do
    Except
        To
           Wait!

Christmas
Marchette Chute

My goodness, my goodness,
It's Christmas again.
The bells are all ringing.
I do not know when
I've been so excited.
The tree is all fixed,
The candles are lighted,
The pudding is mixed.
The wreath's on the door,
And the carols are sung.
The presents are wrapped,
And the holly is hung.
The turkey is sitting
All safe in its pan,
And I am behaving
As calm as I can.

The Little Lights of Christmas
Polly Prindle

I love the lights of Christmas,
The candleflame that gleams
From clear unshaded windows
In golden-threaded streams.

I love each bulb that glistens
On every spicy tree,

And every star seems brighter
At Christmastime to me.

But the little lamps that thrill me
From earth up to the skies
Are the little lights of Christmas
That shine in children's eyes.

A Child's Face
Virginia Covey Boswell

Christmas is a child's face
Watching from the stair,
Peeking through the banisters
At magic everywhere.

Christmas is a child's face,
Rosy, deep with love;
Trusting, like the Wise Men
In the star above.

Christmas is a child's face
Shining soft and dear;
Believing with such rapture
In a cherished time of year.

Christmas comes in many ways
In many homes apart,
But always it's a Child's face
Shining in your heart.

Photograph by Jessie Walker

Lighting the Way

Joan Donaldson

Several years ago, my mother bought a condominium and prepared to move from her house. When my family visited that fall, she asked, "Would you like these Christmas lights? I'm going to scale back."

We didn't need more lights, but the strand in her hand had encircled the living room window of my childhood home. Those small, multi-colored lights had greeted me when I returned from the end of college terms and had sparkled through the holidays.

"And here are a couple of ornaments from your grandmother, plus the one you made as a toddler."

Alongside the antique glass lantern lay an English walnut partially covered with crumpled tinfoil attached to a loop of blue velvet ribbon. The crinkled foil reminded me of the satin-covered Styrofoam balls that my young sons had decorated with glue, glitter, and sequins.

"Thank you," I said, holding another segment of my childhood.

The Sunday before Christmas, my husband, John, and our sons piled pine boughs and spruce branches on sleds. We hauled them home across the snow-covered pasture along with a small pine we dug for the boys. John draped the boughs along the length of the beam that runs down the center of our timber-frame house, and the scent of pine filled the room. I unpacked boxes of ornaments that my family and friends had made over the years—paper-cut rabbits, felt angels, and quilted stars. We threaded strings of lights and tinsel across the boughs; but when we finished, the lights my mother had given me still sat on the table. We glanced at the boys' tree smothered in paper chains, satin balls, and silver icicles.

"No more room for these," said John.

"I suppose I could tape them around a window," I said.

"Can I have them?" seven-year-old Carlos asked.

"Sure." I figured our son would decorate his room, perhaps hang the lights around the bunk beds. But that evening when father and sons went out to milk the goats and collect eggs, Carlos took along the lights and a roll of duct tape.

Thirty minutes later, John stomped snow off his boots. "Did you look outside?"

I rubbed steam from the kitchen window and stared at the red, blue, green, and yellow lights framing the chicken-coop window. The snow reflected the bright bulbs in a watercolor wash.

"Think the chickens will lay more eggs?" Carlos asked.

"I'm sure they will," I answered.

For some reason, Carlos never repeated that capricious act. But years later, after John and I had arranged icicle lights along the front of our house, we still had a couple of strands left. We stood holding them in the December twilight.

"Well," John said. "They'd look good on the goat barn."

Our eyes met, remembering a roll of duct tape and a black-haired boy who would soon complete his first term at college. Ever since that Christmas, icicle lights sway along the eaves of our goat barn, casting chips of color across the snow, lighting the path home.

Barn door in Arkansas Valley, Colorado. Photograph by Michael DeYong/Alaska Stock LLC/Alamy

Christmas Lights

Mamie Ozburn Odum

They shine in spires and windows golden;
Myriads of lights like curtains rise.
In the festooned tree, the stars enfolden
Reflect the softened beauty of the skies.

Homes are bedecked in all their glory,
With twinkling lights above the arching door;
The shadows in the distance hover
As tree-decked hues sparkle the more.

The Christmas lights like gems are glowing,
Encased in quaintest filigree,
While softened winter winds are blowing
The chimes of Christmas bells to me.

And as the bright lights shine and glisten
And children sing, O lovely band,
"Glory to God in the Highest,"
The caroling notes spread o'er the land.

And as we join the past and future,
Our hearts in sweet remembrance rise.
No deed can dim the glorious vision,
For the sweet old story never dies.

Gazebo in Hebron, New Hampshire.
Photograph by William H. Johnson

Our Treasured Traditions

Putting Up the Tree

Lesley Conger

We always take our tree down on New Year's Eve; and since we always put it up on Christmas Eve, this makes us the last family in the neighborhood to put a tree up and the first to take it down. We've been battling the children on this score for years, while the tree lights go on in window after window up and down the street. They would have us putting it up earlier and earlier until, I suppose, it would be the first thing we'd do after finally persuading them to throw out the Halloween jack-o'-lantern with the top of his skull hung with long green and gray mold and his face caved in with a puckering, toothless, centenarian smile. But we've held out, even against charges of being the meanest parents in town.

Of course, a dry Christmas tree is a fire hazard. But if you take a look at our garage with the car parked in front of it because we can't get it inside, you'll know we aren't really concerned with such a practical reason. The truth is that I can't bear to get up in the morning and start a new year with last year's tree standing there in the living room in a shaft of pale, wintry sun, looking like somebody who just got home from an all-night party—disheveled, exhausted, and footsore. It isn't that we don't like Christmas trees; we just don't want to be tired of ours before we take it down.

So we put the tree up on Christmas Eve.

Every other year or so, another child is old enough to join the ritual, another child emancipated and wise with the knowledge that Santa Claus is really Mommy and Daddy and everybody who loves you—and wishing, wistfully, that he weren't, or at least that enlightenment could have been put off just one more year. (But, as childhood's traumatic experiences go, this may not be so much worse than finding out that the plastic model submarine that looks about a foot long on the outside of the cereal package is really the size of the first two joints of your little finger; and it may be that even a six-year-old child can perceive, in his heart if not in his head, what lies behind each of the two deceptions.)

As for the tree, it is always a Douglas fir, *Pseudotsuga taxifolia*, no exceptions allowed; always as big as possible; and always green. I vaguely recall from years ago a season of aberration, probably adolescent, when I was convinced we ought to have a silver tree with blue ornaments only, but my mother must have prevailed; she could still remember the huge *Weihnachtsbaum* her father and older brothers would drag into the big room of the combination saloon-and-inn the family owned. It was enormous to begin with, but if it were not plump or symmetrical enough to suit them, they would even graft in additional branches to fill it out to perfection. What miserable spindly evergreen sprayed with a silver disguise and hung with ice-cold blue could compete with the memory of such a tree reaching to the ceiling, smelling of the forest, and quivering with the splendid, dangerous light of candles?

We put our tree up with tremendous seriousness, moving the colored lights from socket to socket and standing back to squint at the effect, worrying about too many reds on one side and too many greens on the other. We hang the balls, lifting each one tenderly from its tissue-paper nest. Some are new, some are older than our oldest child, but there is one neither gold nor silver nor any of the shiny, gaudy colors. It is a satin white with soft green leaves and a velvet peach, and this one I remember from my own childhood; and I hang it myself, trembling each year for fear it might fall and break and my heart with it. Then there are little birds to clip on the branches, and a tiny wooden angel, and candy canes and—in years when I am ambitious—decorated cookies with loops of thread to hang them by, and strings of popcorn and cranberries.

The last thing to go on the tree is the silver rain. I know it says "icicles" on the package, but I have lived most of my life in this immoderately moderate northwest climate, and to me it always looks like rain. We hang the rain patiently, precisely, strand by strand, and anyone who starts to take it heedlessly by the handful and throw it at the tree (a degraded practice followed in some savage quarters) is immediately apprehended with cries of horror and revulsion. But, at last, the sheet is spread beneath the tree; and one of the boys crouches there in readiness, holding the light plug while the rest of us switch off the lamps. A prickly moment of darkness—and we all sigh in unison our skyrocket-bursting, Christmas-tree-lighting-up sigh: "Aaaahhhhh!"

Trimming the Tree

Wilma Willett Fuchs

Again we trim the Christmas tree
And gaily deck each bough,
A loving task of many years
As it was then, 'tis now.

We set the tree in holder firm,
Next fasten each small light,
And then upon the topmost point
We place the star of white.

We drape the tree with ropes of gold
And shining silver strands,
And then upon each branch we hang
Old ornaments so grand.

Our task complete, we reminisce
About our trees long past.
We loved them all, yet vow this one
Is nicer than the last.

And as we gather round the tree,
Remembering other years,
There is a glisten in our eyes,
Perhaps from joy, from tears.

And while reflections of the past
Set every tree apart,
That same old Christmas spirit
Is reflected in each heart.

Expressions of Love

Phyllis Ruth Chapman

Last night, feeling a happy glow after trimming our tree for Christmas, we were talking about why we love Christmas so much.

Why do people rush about, complaining about the bustle and the time and money spent, and yet they secretly love every shining minute of it? We decided it is because at this season, old and young alike come closer to living our Savior's teaching—"Love one another"—than at any time of the year. Indeed, the concentrated love being generated in homes all over our land should create a glow in the sky like the northern lights. Everything we do for Christmas is an expression of love: when we make a gift, as we take each careful stitch, or stir, or paint, we think with tenderness of the one for whom it is meant. As we decorate our homes, inside and out, we are giving the gift of beauty to all who see. As we shop for the just-right present for each one on our list, each minute of time spent is a gift of love too. When we address Christmas cards, we are sending a little bit of ourselves to say, "I love you. I wish I could tell you myself, but let this little messenger do it for me." The smiles we give as we hurry about are for love and say, "Merry Christmas!" and "God be with you!"

O blessed Christmas! It is too bad your message of love can't last all year. But how wonderful that we dedicate ourselves to spreading His love for this one joyous season that brings old friends nearer and makes new friends dearer.

Thank God for Christmas—the birth day, the gift of His Son who loved us so much that He spent His too-short life teaching us to love one another and then died for us. May the loving spirit of Christmas stay a glowing ember in our hearts always.

THROUGH MY WINDOW

Homemade Holidays

Pamela Kennedy

Some of my favorite Christmas memories feature homemade gifts. When I was a little girl growing up in the 1950s, I remember the excitement on Christmas morning when I peeked at the tree to see what Santa had brought. It somehow never seemed odd to me that Santa's best gifts were always something my mother had created! One year there was a doll bed complete with handmade sheets, embroidered pillowcases, and a ruffled canopy and coverlet of yellow organdy. Another year I received a pink and white metal doll case filled with a wardrobe for my Revlon doll—every outfit, from lounging pajamas to a brocade formal, hand-crafted by my mother.

When I was older, I recall helping Mom make homemade candles and buttery caramel popcorn balls to give to neighbors and friends at Christmastime. And I also remember the joy of delivering the gifts as well as the special pride of saying, "I made it myself!" I'm not sure it ever occurred to me that much of the motivation for my mother's creative generosity was economic. But because there wasn't much extra money to spend on extravagant Christmas presents, she found another way to be extravagant—with her effort and love. And perhaps that was the lesson she taught me as I stood beside her on a step stool, pouring melted wax into molds or tying red ribbons around the popcorn balls: time says love more eloquently than money.

When my husband and I were first married, I determined to follow in my mother's footsteps. I announced that I would make our Christmas gifts. Coming from a long line of shoppers, he was a bit skeptical about my plan. I think he had visions of cardboard manger scenes or craft projects from his Boy Scout days. "Trust me," I said, with a bit more confidence than I felt at the time. "They'll love them."

It was the early 1970s, and knit clothing was popular; so I signed up for a "Stretch 'n' Sew" course at a local fabric shop. That Christmas, everyone on our list got handmade T-shirts. I did polos, pullovers, and even a pretty spiffy velour top for my mother-in-law. The next year I created full-length robes for our moms and spent hours embroidering and framing family coats of arms for our dads.

When our children came along, I sewed huge stuffed dogs for the boys one year and a box of dress-up clothes for our daughter. The year that Cabbage Patch dolls were all the rage (and sold out in every store!), I found a pattern and created not only the dolls but also sets of matching pajamas for them and the kids.

When our home was full of teenagers, life was so busy it was often November before I started

Photograph by Brian Hagiwara/FoodPix/Getty Images, Inc.

thinking about Christmas gifts each year, and then there was too little time left to plan and create homemade gifts. It was easier to shop from catalogs, online, or at the mall. But I found I missed the joy of creating something by hand, of seeing the special appreciation reserved for a homemade gift, and the pleasure of saying, "I made it myself!"

Then, a couple of years ago, I was cleaning out a closet and found boxes of old photos. They needed organizing—or tossing out! But as I sat one summer afternoon going through them, an idea bloomed. I'd create an album chronicling the life of each of our adult children. It took the better part of a month, but the results were worth it. On Christmas morning, when the children opened their albums, everything stopped for about an hour as they leafed through the pages, laughing and telling stories about the different ages and stages of their lives. I felt that old joy again as they hugged me and thanked me for giving them something I had made myself.

And now *they* have started creating homemade gifts for Christmas! Perhaps it has something to do with the economy, or maybe it's just about being more connected. Whatever the reason, I'm delighted! My daughter concocted a selection of luxurious natural body scrubs from sugar and essential oils and packaged them in attractive jars salvaged from thrift shops. For months, each time I showered, I felt pampered and loved, enveloped in a steaming cloud of fragrant lavender or spicy orange. Last year she presented us with tins of homemade truffles in a variety of scrumptious flavors from coconut to salty almond. When our son and daughter-in-law showed up after a cross-country flight, they

unpacked gifts wrapped in hand-decorated paper. But the wrappings weren't the only things that were handmade. Buttery shortbread cookies and jars of sugared citrus rind filled one box and a beautifully hand-knit scarf tumbled out of another. "We made them ourselves!" they declared, as we licked the crumbs from our fingers.

I think we treasure these gifts from hand and heart so much because it requires a sacrifice greater than money to create them. It takes time: time to think about what might please the receiver, time to gather the supplies, time to create the gift itself. I recall seeing a small plaque hanging in a friend's home that said, "Love is spelled T-I-M-E." And I guess that's it in a nutshell. When I open a handmade gift, it reassures me that Christmas is still about the kind of love that is counted more in hours than dollars. I'm glad we've come full circle.

Bits & Pieces

May you have the greatest two gifts
of all on these holidays: someone to
love and someone who loves you.
—*John Sinor*

The most splendid Christmas gift, the most
marveled and magic, is the gift that has not
yet been opened. Opaque behind wrapping
or winking foil, is a box full of possibilities.
—*George Easterbrook*

May no gift be too small to give,
nor too simple to receive, which
is wrapped in thoughtfulness
and tied with love.
—*L. O. Baird*

One doesn't forget the rounded wonder
in the eyes of a boy as he comes bursting
upstairs on Christmas morning and finds
the two-wheeler or fire truck of which
for weeks he scarcely dared dream.

—*Max Lerner*

The Magi, as you know, were
Wise Men—wonderfully wise men—
who brought gifts to the Babe in
the manger. They invented the art
of giving Christmas presents.

—*O. Henry*

Giving presents is a talent—
to know what a person wants,
to know when and how to get it,
to give it lovingly and well.

—*Pamela Glenconner*

December gifts—
custom, ceremony,
celebration, consecration—
come to us wrapped up, not
in tissue and ribbons, but in
cherished memories.

—*Sarah Ban Breathnach*

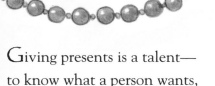

Home for Christmas

Elizabeth Bowen

*T*his is meeting-time again. Home is the magnet. The winter land roars and hums with the eager speed of return journeys. The dark is noisy and bright with late-night arrivals—doors thrown open, running shadows on snow, open arms, kisses, voices, and laughter—laughter at everything and nothing. Inarticulate, giddying, and confused are those original minutes of being back again. The very familiarity of everything acts like shock. Contentment has to be drawn in slowly, steadyingly, in deep breaths—there is so much of it. We rely on home not to change, and it does not, wherefore we give thanks. Again Christmas: the abiding point of return. Set apart by its mystery, mood, and magic, the season seems in a way to stand outside time. All that is dear, that is lasting, renews its hold on us: we are home again. . . .

Each Christmas, we have garnered in yet another year; to be glad, to celebrate to the full, we are come together. How akin we are to each other, how speechlessly dear and one in the fundamentals of being; Christmas shows us. No other time grants us, quite, this vision—round the tree or gathered before the fire we perceive anew, with joy, one another's faces. And each time faces come to mean more.

Is it not one of the mysteries of life that should, after all, be so simple? Yes, as simple as Christmas, simple as this—journeys through the dark to a lighted door, arms open; laughter-smothered kisses, kiss-smothered laughter; and blessedness in the heart of it all. Here are the verities, all made gay with tinsel! Dear, silly Christmas-card saying and cracker mottoes—let them speak! Or, since we cannot speak, let us sing! Dearer than memory, brighter than expectation is the ever returning *now* of Christmas. Why else, each time we greet its return, should happiness ring out in us like a peal of bells?

Hampden Community in Baltimore, Maryland. Photograph by Greg Pease/Photographer's Choice/Getty Images, Inc.

The House That Is Your Heart

James Dillet Freeman

Now take this Christmas Day to go
A little way apart,
And with your gentle hands prepare
The house that is your heart.

Brush out the dusty fears, brush out
The cobwebs of your care,
Till, in the house that is your heart,
It's Christmas everywhere.

Light every window up with love
And let that love shine through,
So they who walk outside may share
The blessed light with you.

Then will the rooms with joy be bright,
With peace the hearth be blessed,
And Christ Himself will enter in
To be your Christmas guest.

NOT A CREATURE WAS STIRRING *by Diane Phalen*

The Angels' Song

Deborah A. Bennett

Listen close some winter's night
and hear the angels' song,
echoing round the moonlit plains
and valleys still and long;

Listen, like the sky is full
of silence and silver stars,
like hillsides lie in sequined snow
and ice from near and far;

Listen, like the quiet creeps
along the panes and eaves,
like frost upon the shoreline grass,
like wind among the trees;

Like shepherds watching o'er their flocks
beside the firelight's glow,
and hear the strains of angels' songs
no matter where you go.

God's Eyes

Deborah A. Bennett

His eyes are on the rooftops
glittering with snow
and watching as the streetlights turn
the sidewalks all aglow.

He sees the wind rattle the gate
and whisper on the sill.
He sees the people shiver by
the silver curbs and hills.

His eyes are on the nests of sparrows
sleeping in the trees.
And looking down between the stars,
He's watching over me.

HOME IS WHERE THE HEART IS *by Sam Timm.*
Image courtesy www.wildwings.com

Hark! The Herald Angels Sang

Evelyn Miller

Christmas was upon me again. In the living room, standing proudly, was a small tree, magnificent with several vintage ornaments (a few last remnants of childhood Christmases), colored lights, and, on the top, a rather bedraggled angel.

Modern electric lights in colors sprayed radiance among the furry branches of the small, long-needled tree—my tree of choice now that I am widowed with children grown and gone. And suddenly, I didn't see my modern tree at all—but another, earlier version.

I see the tree of my childhood. I am ten years old, and the year is 1924. I am very excited, for it is Christmas Eve. I am walking through deep snow; and the swirling, soft flakes touch my hot cheeks. I toss back my stylish, carefully rolled finger curls and brush the snowflakes from my eyelashes as I continue to wend my way from the very end of Fifth Street, where I live, on the south side of our small city of Grand Haven, Michigan. Upon reaching the corner of Franklin Street and Fifth, I abruptly turn left. One more block to go.

Ah, there it is, barely visible now in the thickening flurry of the soft snowflakes—the church of my childhood, the St. John's Evangelical Lutheran Church of my German ancestors. I am the youngest member of the family in the church of my elders.

My fingers tingle, my cheeks grow more rosy, and my heart pounds. It is Christmas Eve; and Christmas Eve is not only the night to usher in the birth of Jesus in our small parish, but an evening of unforgettable treats.

As I shyly enter the church, I wistfully look for a place that will give me a complete view of the glorious, towering Christmas tree. My heart almost stops. There it is, in the corner, directly to the right of the tall pulpit at which I hardly dare glance; from it come sermons of such intensity that I cringe inwardly and the gold tassels on the blue velvet paraments seem to shake. But tonight should bring a gentler message—the birth of Christ.

I cannot swallow as I gaze with wonder upon the giant tree. It spans the beams above. Glistening garlands circle it in dignity. And, ah, the candles—beautiful, real candles held in metal cups, standing proudly lighted, interspersed among the prickly branches.

I take my seat and humbly bow my head in prayer. The service begins with the songs I've grown to love, aided by the small choir—"Silent Night"; "Hark, the Herald Angels Sing"; "Oh, Little Town of Bethlehem." As my voice peals out in childish notes, I am filled with glory; and still the best is yet to come.

The minister takes his rightful place in the tall pulpit, and once more we bow in prayer. Although his message is vibrating, inspired, and dedicated, and the old story, new once more, is thrilling, an anticipatory chill runs through me.

Christmas treat time is next! As each child's name is called, that child solemnly takes his place at the front of the church, directly to the left of the tree. One of the elders brings forth a large pack, and one by one, the children file by as their names are called out.

I almost faint as I realize that I am next.

Timidly reaching forth, I am given a small cardboard box filled with hard candies. Lovely Christmas designs are emblazoned on the small box, and a tiny red cord string is attached to the top . . . but there is more!

A mammoth, spicy, dark orange is put into my eager hands. Ah, how the smell permeates the air! My mouth waters.

I go back to my seat and place the candy and orange next to me, for the festivities are not yet over. The more theatrical children who know no shyness now step forward, one by one, and speak Christmas verses. I am next to the last, and I can hardly wait, for I love any type of theatrics.

I am the only one given a Christmas verse with gestures, and joyously I raise my hand, pointing while declaring, "Yonder lies, under the Star of Bethlehem, the crib containing the Baby Jesus." When I speak the name "Baby Jesus," my arms softly form a circle, and I mentally hold the tiny Baby in my eager arms.

There is applause, and it delights me; for then I know I have put my verse over, and it is appreciated and felt. I have made my small contribution to wonderful Baby Jesus and His miraculous birth. I go back and sit down.

Another prayer is offered up after the Christmas collection plate has been passed, and then the final hymns roll forth in beautiful, rich, vibrant tones as the rolling sounds of the church

organ accompany the singers. . . . Triumphant! Triumphant!

Putting my coat on and my woolen cap and gloves and scarf, I anxiously feel for my "treasures" and, grasping them, I leave. When I go out the front door, I once more turn and lovingly survey the triumphant, giant Christmas tree with its flickering candles casting shadows upon the darkened interior.

The snow is now coming down in heavy swirls. Pushing ahead eagerly, I make my way faster and faster back through the footsteps made by others ahead of me.

Turning the corner to the right on Franklin Street, I remake my former steps, in reverse this time. As I approach Washington Street, I glance up at the town clock, which is softly striking the hour of ten PM.

Bells are ringing. . . . The snow is drifting, and a feeling of supreme ecstacy comes over me. . . . It is heavenly.

Christmas Assembly

Mary Lou Carney

Today is the Christmas
   assembly.

I sit with other parents
on brown metal chairs,
all watching the orchestra
file into the gym
wondering when our children
became so tall
   so grown-up
      so serious.

Fluorescent lights glint off
brightly polished baritones
highly buffed cellos.

Stuffy air is shattered by
scrambled sounds of squeals
   and plinks
rumbling groans of bows
drawn across taut strings
as each musician
tackles the task of tuning.

The conductor steps onto
the small black platform,
flanked by poinsettias and pine.
Silence.
His baton hovers in the air
like a mute hummingbird.
Every eye is his.

The baton moves lightly;
the music begins—
filling the gym with
stirring strains of
   remembered carols
melodic magic of
   well-orchestrated parts
and I silently celebrate
the birth of Christ
who
   tunes
     orchestrates
       conducts
my life.

Photograph © moodboard/SuperStock

One Day at a Time

Cindy La Ferle

I still remember my first Advent calendar. Crafted from cardboard and embellished with gold and silver glitter, it was covered with twenty-five tiny perforated windows to be opened daily until Christmas. Behind each window was a small illustration associated with the Nativity in Bethlehem—a blond angel with a trumpet, a Wise Man bearing a gift, or a shepherd with a lamb.

My best friend in grade school was a devout Catholic and seasoned authority on the proper use of Advent calendars. As she often reminded me, the windows could be opened only on their designated dates. Sneaking a peek at the future was strictly prohibited.

Being a practical Presbyterian at the time, I could see nothing sinful in staying ahead of schedule. By the second week of Advent, I knew what was behind every door and window, including the largest and final one that revealed the Baby Jesus in his straw-stuffed manger. Once I did this, of course, I'd completely spoiled my own fun. Half the beauty of an Advent calendar, after all, is the magical sense of wonder and anticipation it provides.

"Most of us think of waiting as something very passive," wrote theologian Henri Nouwen in "Waiting for God," an essay on Advent. "Active waiting means to be fully present to the moment, in the conviction that something is happening where you are and that you want to be present to it."

Henri Nouwen was right. But it took years and several more Advent calendars for the richer lessons of the season—including patience—to take root in my heart. It didn't help that I grew up in the era of instant gratification, when the plots of my favorite TV shows concluded neatly in less than a half hour. Later, as a multi-tasking newlywed with a home of my own, I zapped countless frozen entrees in a microwave before I learned how to cook family meals from scratch. And after a day at the office, I'd always return my phone messages in the kitchen while using my free hand to pull clean dishes from my automatic dishwasher.

I rarely took time to be "fully present to the moment."

Thankfully, I rediscovered the Advent calendar early in my motherhood. Not only did it provide an opportunity to teach my little boy the real reason we give presents for Christmas, it also prompted some meaty discussions on delayed gratification.

I still recall the November afternoon at the local bookstore where my son and I chose his first glitter-splashed Advent calendar. Brushing my hand across the new, shrink-wrapped calendar, I announced that each window must be opened on its designated date. One day at a time. There were still a few days remaining in November, so we would have to wait a few more days before opening the first window.

In the car on the way home, I also explained the long-term benefits of being patient, of being still long enough to appreciate the blessing of each day as it comes. It wasn't an easy lecture for a wiggly five-year-old whose small fingers were itching to tear into the plastic wrap and open all the calendar windows at once. I lightened up a little when I remembered the temptation of fresh glitter and new cardboard. I remembered how it felt to be a child with a fresh sense of wonder.

In retrospect, it's possible that my son took the lesson to heart. Or it could be that he grew bored with the calendar and decided to focus on his holiday wish list. Either way, he never opened a window out of sequence, and the Nativity illustration under our final window was ceremoniously revealed on Christmas morning.

My son is grown and in a home of his own now, but every year I display a favorite Advent calendar showing images of Mary and Jesus from great works of art. Like the ancient icons I've admired in historic churches throughout Europe, the calendar also serves as a reminder to slow down and make time for reverence. Each window invites contemplation of the blessed mother in Bethlehem who gave birth to the Son we honor on December 25— a woman who understood the ultimate reward of waiting.

A Christmas Thought

Margaret E. Sangster

The sweetest gift the Father's love
Sent ever down to men
Came in the stillness and the dark
That thrilled to music when
All suddenly the hills grew bright
And flamed athwart the sky
(A rift of heaven across the night)
The glory from on high.

Strong angels swept their
    hearts of fire
And sang of peace to men;
The wondering shepherds
    heard in awe
And took their pathway then
Along the hills by crag and steep
To find the mother-maid,
In whose glad arms that wintry night
God's gift of gifts was laid.

All heaven was in sweet
    Mary's heart;
The Babe had brought it her.
She did not think it strange to see
The frankincense and myrrh,
The shining gold, the sages gave,
As poured beneath a throne,
In honor of the kingly one,
That hour her very own.

So helpless, yet so beautiful,
Heaven's gift, the undefiled,
Earth's proudest and earth's lowliest
Bowed down before the Child.
And back to heaven the angels went
Whose songs had cleft the night,
And Bethlehem's star was lost amid
The morning's rapturous light.

Heaven's royal gift to
    earth that day,
Heaven's gift of life and love,
Was just a helpless little Child
A mother bent above.
Worth more than ransom ever paid
In weight of gold or gem,
The Child who came to ransom us—
The Babe of Bethlehem.

And, aye, in many an
    earthly home
God's sweetest gift and best
Is still a little child who sleeps
Upon a mother's breast.
And over every cradled head
The angels sing today,
With something of the
    sweetness once
That thrilled the Bethlehem way.

Lo! The Light!

Elizabeth Landeweer

Above the manger stood a star,
A star all wondrous white;
And all about His lowly bed
There welled a flood of light.

It bathed the stable in its glow;
It shone round Mary's head.
And on the kneeling shepherds' cloaks
Its radiant beams were shed.

Star of the world! Through time and space
It flames in glory bright
To make man's pathway through the years
A pilgrimage of light.

It shines for us—that light still shines!
No cloud can dim its spark;
Its radiance blossoms bright with joy,
A beacon in the dark.

The path leads on, the path leads up;
We walk it mile by mile,
And lo! The light His love has lit
Grows brighter all the while.

Oh, never doubt it shines for you,
Though skies seem dark and low.
Keep looking up, keep lifted up—
Somewhere a star will show!

Let not your heart be trouble-filled.
The darkest night must clear,
And life be glad and life be sweet,
For lo! The light is here!

Christmas tree glowing under the northern lights, Sherwood Park,
Alberta, Canada. Photograph © Design Pics/SuperStock

A Controversial Carol

Pamela Kennedy

When we think of beautiful Christmas music, one of the first pieces that comes to mind is "O Holy Night." The imagery and melody of this lovely carol sweep us back to that long ago night of mystery, beauty, and peace. Few of us realize, however, that this Christmas song has a history filled with controversy. It was once not only banned by the clergy in France but also sparked political animosity in the United States!

It all started in 1847 with a French Catholic priest in Roquemaure who wanted an original poem for his Christmas Eve midnight mass. The local commissionaire of wines, Placide Cappeau, was also a gifted poet; and even though Cappeau wasn't the most devout parishioner, the priest respected his talent and asked him to compose some appropriate verses. On a train to Paris shortly thereafter, the poet penned the verses of a poem he titled "Cantique de Noël." Contemplating his verses, Cappeau decided they would be even more impressive if set to music. After arriving in Paris, he met with his friend and composer, Adolphe Charles Adam, a well-known creator of popular operas and ballets. His recent successes with the ballets *Faust* and *Giselle* had made Adam something of a Parisian celebrity. Although not a Christian, Adam was intrigued with his friend's Christmas verses and accepted

Photograph © Nancy Matthews

the challenge to create a melody to complement the poem. Within a few days, he produced an original composition for Cappeau.

Upon his return to Roquemaure, Cappeau presented the finished Christmas song to the priest, who was delighted with both the beautiful melody and heartfelt words. Three weeks later, "Cantique de Noël" debuted in the parish church on Christmas Eve and gained instant popularity.

Within a few years, it became a popular part of Christmas services throughout France.

Back in Roquemaure, however, all was not well. The song's author split with the Catholic Church and joined France's socialist movement. Subsequent to Cappeau's defection from the faith, church leaders discovered that Adam, the song's composer, was Jewish and had written popular stage works they deemed inappropriate entertainment for Christians. These findings prompted the conservative religious establishment to condemn "Cantique de Noël," claiming it possessed a "total absence of the spirit of religion." Although they banned the carol from church services, the clergy had little influence upon the general populace, and French Christians, undaunted by the Church's declaration, continued to sing the beloved carol in their homes and on the streets. Soon, musicians had exported "Cantique de

Noël" all over Europe and even across the Atlantic to the United States.

There, in 1855, John Sullivan Dwight, a Unitarian minister and ardent abolitionist from Massachusetts, was busy developing new material for church hymnals. Happening upon Cappeau's carol, Dwight recognized within its lyrics a message that resonated not only with his theology but also with his political views regarding freedom and equality: "Truly He taught us to love one another; His law is love and His gospel is peace. Chains shall He break, for the slave is our brother; and in His name all oppression shall cease!" Dwight translated the French lyrics into English and renamed the hymn "O Holy Night." As one might expect, the carol gained almost immediate popularity in the pre–Civil War North. In the Confederate South, however, it was a different story. The song's message was deemed subversive and inflammatory, and it would be many years before it was included in Christmas services there.

Now, over 150 years later, this beloved carol is a Christmas tradition in most services around the globe. Amid current challenges and conflicts, its message rings especially true as it draws our attention to the ongoing and universal quest for peace and equality. In the inspiring verses of "O Holy Night" we hear a hope that transcends the Christmas season and looks beyond it to a time when love and compassion might one day rule the whole world.

"O Holy Night"

Lyrics by Placide Cappeau (1808-1877), music by Adolphe Adam (1802-1856),
English translation by John Sullivan Dwight (1813-1893)

O holy night! The stars are brightly shining;
It is the night of our dear Savior's birth.
Long lay the world in sin and error pining,
Till He appeared and the soul felt its worth.
A thrill of hope, the weary world rejoices,
For yonder breaks a new and glorious morn.
Fall on your knees! O, hear the angel voices!
O night divine, O night when Christ was born;
O night, O holy night, O night divine!

Truly He taught us to love one another;
His law is love and His gospel is peace.
Chains He shall break, for the slave is our brother;
And in His name all oppression shall cease!
Sweet hymns of joy in grateful chorus raise we,
With all our hearts we praise His holy name.
Christ is the Lord! Then ever, ever praise we,
His power and glory ever more proclaim!
His power and glory ever more proclaim!

BEHOLD, I BRING YOU TIDINGS OF GREAT JOY *by Tom duBois. Image from Somerset Licensing*

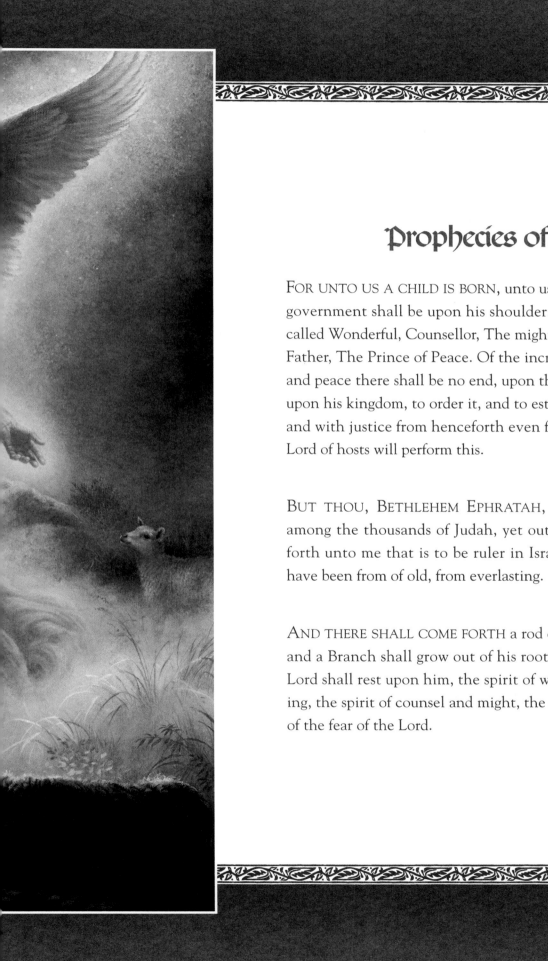

Prophecies of Old

FOR UNTO US A CHILD IS BORN, unto us a son is given: and the government shall be upon his shoulder: and his name shall be called Wonderful, Counsellor, The mighty God, The everlasting Father, The Prince of Peace. Of the increase of his government and peace there shall be no end, upon the throne of David, and upon his kingdom, to order it, and to establish it with judgment and with justice from henceforth even for ever. The zeal of the Lord of hosts will perform this.

—*Isaiah 9:6–7*

BUT THOU, BETHLEHEM EPHRATAH, though thou be little among the thousands of Judah, yet out of thee shall he come forth unto me that is to be ruler in Israel; whose goings forth have been from of old, from everlasting.

—*Micah 5:2*

AND THERE SHALL COME FORTH a rod out of the stem of Jesse, and a Branch shall grow out of his roots: And the spirit of the Lord shall rest upon him, the spirit of wisdom and understanding, the spirit of counsel and might, the spirit of knowledge and of the fear of the Lord.

—*Isaiah 11:1–2*

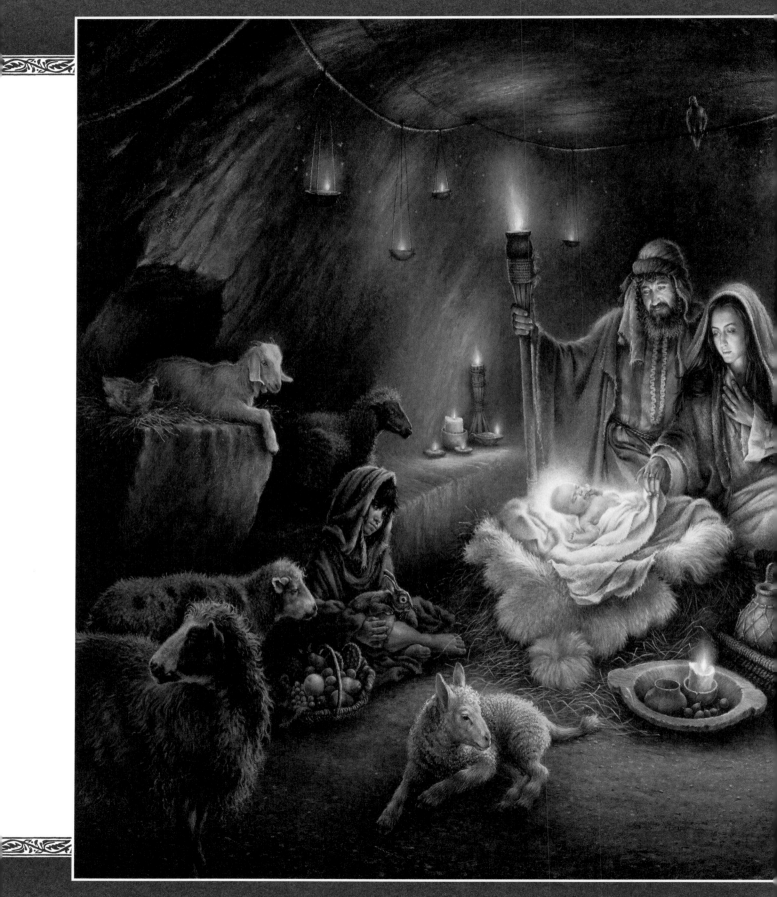

No Room in the Inn *by Tom duBois. Image from Somerset Licensing*

Tidings of Great Importance

Matthew 1:18–25

NOW THE BIRTH OF JESUS CHRIST was on this wise: When as his mother Mary was espoused to Joseph, before they came together, she was found with child of the Holy Ghost.

Then Joseph her husband, being a just man, and not willing to make her a publick example, was minded to put her away privily. But while he thought on these things, behold, the angel of the Lord appeared unto him in a dream, saying, Joseph, thou son of David, fear not to take unto thee Mary thy wife: for that which is conceived in her is of the Holy Ghost. And she shall bring forth a son, and thou shalt call his name JESUS: for he shall save his people from their sins.

Now all this was done, that it might be fulfilled which was spoken of the Lord by the prophet, saying, Behold, a virgin shall be with child, and shall bring forth a son, and they shall call his name Emmanuel, which being interpreted is, God with us.

Then Joseph being raised from sleep did as the angel of the Lord had bidden him, and took unto him his wife: And knew her not till she had brought forth her firstborn son: and he called his name JESUS.

Seekers from the East

Matthew 2:1–12

NOW WHEN JESUS WAS BORN in Bethlehem of Judaea in the days of Herod the king, behold, there came wise men from the east to Jerusalem, Saying, Where is he that is born King of the Jews? for we have seen his star in the east, and are come to worship him.

When Herod the king had heard these things, he was troubled, and all Jerusalem with him. And when he had gathered all the chief priests and scribes of the people together, he demanded of them where Christ should be born.

And they said unto him, In Bethlehem of Judaea: for thus it is written by the prophet, And thou Bethlehem, in the land of Juda, art not least among the princes of Juda: for out of thee shall come a Governor, that shall rule my people Israel.

Then Herod, when he had privily called the wise men, enquired of them diligently what time the star appeared.

And he sent them to Bethlehem, and said, Go and search diligently for the young child; and when ye have found him, bring me word again, that I may come and worship him also. When they had heard the king, they departed; and, lo, the star, which they saw in the east, went before them, till it came and stood over where the young child was.

When they saw the star, they rejoiced with exceeding great joy.

And when they were come into the house, they saw the young child with Mary his mother, and fell down, and worshipped him: and when they had opened their treasures, they presented unto him gifts; gold, and frankincense, and myrrh.

And being warned of God in a dream that they should not return to Herod, they departed into their own country another way.

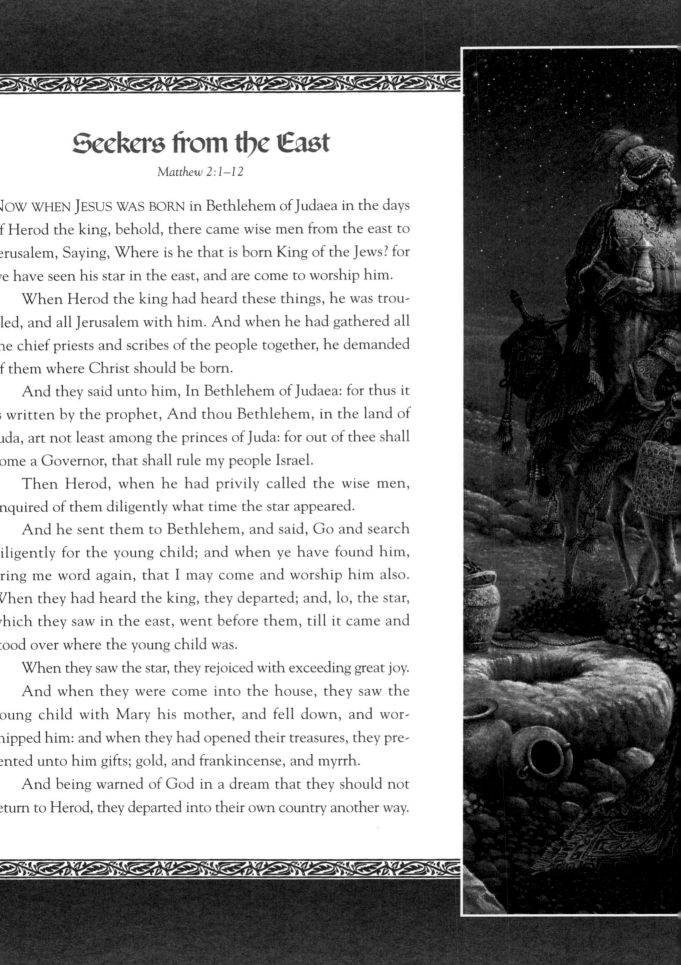

AND THE WISE MEN CAME BEARING GIFTS *by Tom duBois. Image from Somerset Licensing*

Let the Stable Still Astonish

Leslie Leyland Fields

Let the stable still astonish:
straw-dirt floor, dull eyes,
dusty flanks of donkeys, oxen;
crumbling, crooked walls;
no bed to carry that pain.
And then, the Child,
rag-wrapped, laid to cry
  in a trough.

Who would have
  chosen this?
Who would have
  said: "Yes,
let the God of all the
  heavens and earth
be born here, in
  this place"?

Who but the same God
who stands in the darker,
  fouler rooms
of our hearts
and says, "Yes, let the God
  of heaven and earth
be born here—
in *this* place."

Barn at dusk in Arkansas Valley, Colorado. Photograph by Michael DeYoung/Alaska Stock LLC/Alamy

It Must Have Been

Ernest C. Wilson

It must have been a silent night
On which the Wise Men trod
The steadfast hills to worship
The infant Son of God.

It must have been a radiant night
On which the star outshone
The brightest stars of all the years
And paused to crown His throne.

It must have been a lonely night
On which the shepherds came
To kneel before a manger bed
And breathe the holy name.

It must have been a holy night
When heaven's legions sang
Their alleluiahs to the Child
Newborn in Bethlehem.

Tonight the sky is hushed and clear,
Bright stars the heaven adorn;
It must have been a night like this
When our Lord Christ was born.

The Christmas Symbol

Author Unknown

Only a manger, cold and bare,
Only a maiden mild,
Only some shepherds kneeling there,
Watching a little Child;
And yet that maiden's arms enfold
The King of heaven above;
And in the Christ Child we behold
The Lord of life and love.

When the Stars of Morning Sang

Anne P. L. Field

When the stars of morning sang
    Long ago,
Sweet the air with music rang
    Through the snow;
There beside the mother mild
Slept the blessed Christmas Child,
Slumber holy, undefiled—
    Here below.

When the Wise Men traveled far
    Through the night,
Following the guiding star
    Pure and bright,

Lo! it stood above the place
Sanctified by Heaven's grace
And upon the Christ Child's face
    Shed its light.

When the world lay hushed and still
    Christmas morn,
Suddenly were skies athrill—
    "Christ is born!"
Angel voices, high and clear,
Chanted tidings of good cheer,
"See, the Infant King is here—
    Christ is born!"

Christmas Song

Bliss Carman

Above the weary waiting world,
Asleep in chill despair,
There breaks a sound of joyous bells upon
    the frosted air.
And o'er the humblest rooftree, lo,
A star is dancing on the snow.

What makes the yellow star to dance
Upon the brink of night?
What makes the breaking dawn to glow

So magically bright,
And all the earth to be renewed
With infinite beatitude?

The singing bells, the throbbing star,
The sunbeams on the snow,
And the awakening heart that leaps,
New ecstasy to know,
They all are dancing in the morn
Because a little Child is born.

Wooster Scott

Were Earth a Thousand Times as Fair

Martin Luther

Were earth a thousand times as fair,
Beset with gold and jewels rare,
She yet were far too poor to be
A narrow cradle, Lord, for Thee.

The Birthday of the Lord

Mary Jane Carr

The Baby Christ, when He
    was born,
Was cradled in a manger.
Still He was King of all the world—
Was ever story stranger?

The shepherds came from far
    and wide
And, wondering, bent above Him;
His will it was that hearts of men
Should know Him and should
    love Him.

The cattle breathed their breath
    on Him;
The little lambs pressed near Him;
His will it was that man nor beast
Should stand apart nor fear Him.

Then let your hearts be filled
    with joy
While Christmas bells are ringing,
And keep the birthday of
    the Lord
With merriment and singing.

Frost-touched holly. Photograph by Flowerphotos © 2010 Masterfile Corporation

Merry Christmas

Margaret Rorke

The sparkle from a pair of eyes
Lit up by Santa's sweet surprise,
A hearty laugh from one himself
Who acts a bit like that old elf,
A healthy home with spicy smells
That blend with pine, a few church bells,

Some cards, a visit from a friend,
A moment that you'll have to spend
Rereading Luke, some carols sung:
All this and more you'll find among
The wishes that I wish your way
To merry-up your Christmas Day.

Readers are invited to submit original poetry and prose for possible use in future publications. Please send no more than four typed submissions to: Magazine Submissions, Ideals Publications, 2630 Elm Hill Pike, Suite 100, Nashville, Tennessee 37214. Manuscripts will be returned if a self-addressed stamped envelope is included.

ISBN-13: 978-0-8249-1325-0

Published by Ideals Publications, a Guideposts Company
Nashville, Tennessee
www.idealsbooks.com

Publisher, Peggy Schaefer
Editor, Melinda L. R. Rumbaugh
Copy Editors, Michelle Prater Burke, Kaye Dacus
Designer, Marisa Jackson
Permissions Editor, Patsy Jay

Cover: *Christmas* by Isabella Angelini. Copyright © 2010 Angelini/ Design Bank/Interlitho/Applejack Art Partners
Inside front cover: Image by John Walter © Ideals Publications
Inside back cover: Image by John Walter © Ideals Publications
Additional Art Credits: Original art for "Family Recipes" and "Bits & Pieces" features by Kathy Rusynyk

ACKNOWLEDGMENTS:

BOWEN, ELIZABETH. "Home for Christmas." Copyright © by Elizabeth Bowen. Reproduced with permission of Curtis Brown Ltd, London on behalf of the Estate of Elizabeth Bowen. CARNEY, MARY LOU. "Christmas Assembly" from *A Month of Mondays.* Copyright © 1984. Published by Abingdon Press. Used by permission of the author. CARR, MARY JANE. "The Birthday of the Lord" from *Top of the Morning* by Mary Jane Carr, copyright © by the author. FREEMAN, JAMES DILLET, "The House That Is Your Heart." Used by permission of the Unity School of Christianity, Unity Village, Missouri. MILLER, EVELYN. "Hark! The Herald Angels Sang" from *Bringing In the Sheaves,* Used by permission of the House of White Birches, Berne, IN, www.GoodOldDaysOnline.com. RORKE, MARGARET L. "Merry Christmas" from *An Old Cracked Cup.* Copyright © 1980 by the author. Used by permission of Margaret Ann Rorke. WILSON, ERNEST C. "It Must Have Been" by Ernest C. Wilson, from *Best Loved Unity Poems,* 1946. Used by permission of the Unity School of Christianity, Unity Village, Missouri.
OUR THANKS to the following authors or their heirs: Deborah A. Bennett, Virginia Covey Boswell, Phyllis Ruth Chapman, Marchette Chute, Elizabeth Collier, Lesley Conger, Joan Donaldson, Leslie Leyland Fields, Rosalyn Hart Finch, Wilma Willett Fuchs, Sudie Stuart Hager, Pamela Kennedy, Lucille King, Cynthia G. La Ferle, Elizabeth Landeweer, Mamie Ozburn Odum, Ree Reaney, and Eileen Spinelli.

Every effort has been made to establish ownership and use of each selection in this book. If contacted, the publisher will be pleased to rectify any inadvertent errors or omissions in subsequent editions.